# Dice Activities for Subtraction

## Engage • Challenge • Empower

**Mary Saltus, Diane Neison, Chet Delani,
Marcia Fitzgerald, Karen Moore**

Printed in the United States of America.

This book is printed on recycled paper.

Order Number 211222
ISBN 978-1-58324-330-5

D E F G H 19 18 17 16 15

395 Main Street
Rowley, MA 01969
www.didax.com

# Dice Activities for Subtraction

## Introduction

Successful math students manipulate numbers mentally. The activities in **Dice Activities for Subtraction** were created by teachers to engage students in developing fluency with the arithmetic operation of subtraction and the mathematical principles involved in thinking about subtraction in multiple ways. The activities are designed to empower students with the ability to address mathematical problems and challenges with a sense of curiosity and confidence.

The preceding books in this series stressed addition and multiplication facts. Research by well-known educational psychologists, including Piaget, has emphasized the challenge of subtraction as a more difficult operation than addition or multiplication for young students. The concept of "something missing" versus combining sums and repeated additions is a struggle for the young child. The activities in this book focus on the subtraction concept of "minus" (take away) as well as the concept of "difference" (comparison), providing ample opportunities to develop fluency with both concepts of subtraction.

These activities focus on the NCTM standards of Number and Operations. They also address the standards of Reasoning, Problem Solving, and Communication. The NCTM standards are the framework for all published mathematic programs as well as state and local curricula frameworks; thus, these activities are easily integrated into a scope and sequence whenever the topic is addressed. In some instances, the teacher will want to replace an activity in the school-based text with one found in this book, as the dice activities are challenging, more apt to produce long-term mastery, and develop an interest in and curiosity about math.

The authors currently use *Dice Activities for Subtraction* as part of their curriculum to train elementary-school teachers in how to teach mathematics. The activities require the use of dice, tiles, or tokens—commonly available classroom manipulatives. They provide an opportunity for students to play with mathematical ideas without paper-and-pencil drill.

Our work is continually expanding and we welcome any suggestions for modification of these activities that will lead to greater mathematical thinking on the part of our students.

—The Authors, mathofcourse@gmail.com

## Contents

## Notes to Teachers

***Dice Activities for Subtraction*** is designed for teachers and parents to use with children in grades 1–3. These engaging, challenging, and fun activities build number sense and generate a conceptual base for number. Children enjoy revisiting the activities and, in doing so, have an opportunity to practice subtraction facts without tedious paper-and-pencil drill.

These dice activities provide opportunities to:

- Develop the concept of the difference between two numbers
- Develop the concept of minus—removing a smaller amount from a larger amount
- Develop fluency with basic subtraction facts
- Reinforce number patterns
- Develop game strategy
- Explore the probability concept of chance
- Develop communication and cooperation skills by working in teams of two students

***Dice Activities for Subtraction*** is organized into eight sections. Each section presents a specific activity.

The **Graph** and **Chart** activities are paired introductory lessons to familiarize students with subtraction concepts. The simplicity of these activities makes each a tool for diversifying learning. Some students may find it beneficial to stay with these activities, developing recognition and fluency, while others are ready for more challenging involvement.

The **Table Completion** activities challenge students to fill in their chart before their opponent. Some **Table Completion** activities involve students working on a different subtrahend than their opponent.

The focus of the **Round** activities is to develop fluency with subtraction facts. Some **Round** activities involve subtracting multiples of 10 and multiples of 5.

Each **Pattern** activity presents four subtraction concepts that focus on developing recognition of subtraction patterns, with some activities emphasizing the ones place in subtracting a subtrahend and others emphasizing the tens place. Four **Table Completions** charts are aligned so that students can make generalizations about the patterns. The patterns are repeated as **Round** activities for students to practice their generalizations.

The repetition throughout the **Differences Between Two Dice** activities facilitates students' ability to quickly recognize the difference in value between two dice.

**Hidden Number,** similar to the game Concentration or Memory, asks students to not only compute the solution to a subtraction fact but also to recall under which tile the solution is hiding. Each concept is presented as a 3 x 4 grid, involving 12 possible hidden numbers, and a more challenging 5 x 5 grid with 25 possible solutions.

Each **Bingo** activity consists of five cards. If students are paired in teams of two, the activity will involve 10 students. One student acts as the "caller," tossing a die or dice and calling out the number. All players involved in the game perform the required computation, and if all agree on the answer, the students look to see if they can place a token on their card. The first team to get bingo wins.

**Tic-Tac-Toe** and **Four-Grid Tic-Tac-Toe** are paired for each concept. **Tic-Tac-Toe** is a game of chance. The players are more dependent on the toss of the dice than in any of the other activities. The Tic-Tac-Toe activities are a simplified introduction to the subtraction concept.

**Four-Grid Tic-Tac-Toe** is less an activity of chance and more of skill than simple Tic-Tac-Toe because players have more opportunities to block their opponents. Players place three tokens in a row on as many grids as they can until all possible moves have been played. Players then count their sets of three tokens in a row to determine who has won.

Blank charts are included with each activity to give teachers and students opportunities to create their own dice activities.

Assigning the same activity but different subtraction concepts for specific students gives teachers opportunities to differentiate class instruction and homework assignments.

Encourage students to think their way through subtraction as a mental activity. If they are subtracting $15 - 4$, for example, ask them to first consider $15 - 5$, which is an easier equation to solve. Explore what they would have to do to use the answer from $15 - 5$ to solve $15 - 4$. If students are struggling with subtraction facts, suggest that they use the Hundred Chart on page vi to help them with their calculations.

# Hundred Chart

| 1 | 2 | 3 | 4 | 5 | 6 | 7 | 8 | 9 | 10 |
|---|---|---|---|---|---|---|---|---|---|
| 11 | 12 | 13 | 14 | 15 | 16 | 17 | 18 | 19 | 20 |
| 21 | 22 | 23 | 24 | 25 | 26 | 27 | 28 | 29 | 30 |
| 31 | 32 | 33 | 34 | 35 | 36 | 37 | 38 | 39 | 40 |
| 41 | 42 | 43 | 44 | 45 | 46 | 47 | 48 | 49 | 50 |
| 51 | 52 | 53 | 54 | 55 | 56 | 57 | 58 | 59 | 60 |
| 61 | 62 | 63 | 64 | 65 | 66 | 67 | 68 | 69 | 70 |
| 71 | 72 | 73 | 74 | 75 | 76 | 77 | 78 | 79 | 80 |
| 81 | 82 | 83 | 84 | 85 | 86 | 87 | 88 | 89 | 90 |
| 91 | 92 | 93 | 94 | 95 | 96 | 97 | 98 | 99 | 100 |

# Subtraction Graph and Chart Activities

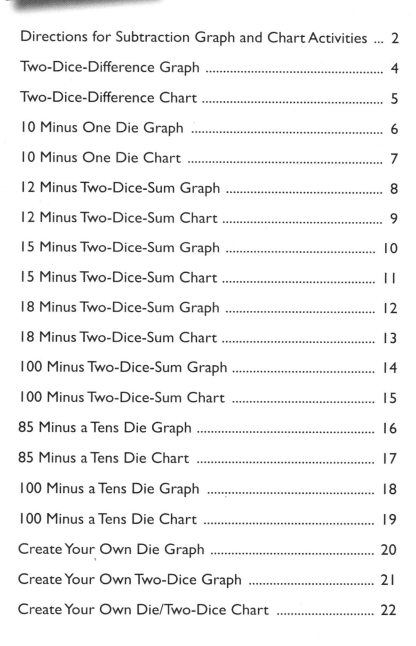

## Contents

# Directions for Subtraction Graph and Chart Activities

**Objectives**

- Develop a sense of number and number patterns when subtracting numbers 0 through 100.
- Recognize number patterns when subtracting from a two-digit number ending in 0.
- Recognize number patterns when subtracting 10 from a two-digit number.
- Practice computing the difference between two numbers from 0 to 100.

The **Graph** and **Chart** activities are introductory lessons to familiarize students with subtraction concepts. The simplicity of the activities makes them a tool for diversifying learning. Some students may find it beneficial to stay with the graph activities, developing recognition and fluency, while others are ready for more challenging involvement.

Introduce the **Subtraction Graph** and **Chart** activities by demonstrating them on an overhead. The activities may be played with 2–3 teams or 2–3 players.

## Materials

- Activity sheet
- Dice
- Pencil

## How to Play

### Subtraction Graph Activities

- Toss 1 or 2 dice depending on the activity.
- Perform the required computation.
- Solutions are in sequence along the bottom row of the graph.
- Find the solution and write it in the box above it, or write the number sentence that produced it. For example, on the **10 Minus One Die Graph**, the player tosses 4 and finds 6 on the graph. In the box above it, the player writes "6" or "10 – 4."
- The first team to fill a column is the winner.

### Subtraction Chart Activities

- Each team tosses a die. The highest number goes first.
- Teams choose a color token (tiles, chips, cubes).
- Taking turns, teams toss 1 or 2 dice depending on the activity and perform the required computation.
- Team members find the difference on the chart and place a token on it.
- If no play is possible, the team loses a turn.
- When each box of the chart is filled, team members count the tokens.
- The team with the most tokens wins.

## Suggestions

- Encourage students to think their way through subtraction as a mental activity. If they are subtracting 15 − 4, have them first consider 15 − 5, which is an easier equation to solve. Explore what they would have to do to use the answer from 15 − 5 to solve 15 − 4.

- If students are struggling with subtraction facts, suggest they use the Hundred Chart (page vi) to help them with their calculations.

## Variations

### Subtraction Graph Activities

- The first team to fill two columns is the winner.

- The first team to fill three columns is the winner.

- The first team to fill every column is the winner.

### Subtraction Chart Activities

- With each toss, the team places a token on every box that shows the difference.

- If a team is unable to place a token on a toss, the team replaces an opponent's token with its own token.

- Each team tosses the die or dice 10 times. The team with the most tokens after 10 tosses wins.

## Discussion

### Subtraction Graph Activities

- When the students have completed their graphs, call attention to the patterns that emerge.

- When finding differences using 2 dice, are some columns more likely to be filled in?

- How does this activity help you learn subtraction facts?

### Subtraction Chart Activities

- Is this a game of luck or skill?

- When you have a choice of where to place a token, how do you decide?

- How does this activity help you learn subtraction facts?

# Two-Dice-Difference Graph

**How to Play**

- *Toss two dice. Find the difference.*
- *Fill in the box above the difference.*

| | | | | | |
|---|---|---|---|---|---|
| | | | | | |
| | | | | | |
| | | | | | |
| | | | | | |
| | | | | | |
| **0** | **1** | **2** | **3** | **4** | **5** |

# Two-Dice-Difference Chart

**How to Play**

- Each team tosses a die. Highest number goes first.
- Teams choose a color token (tiles, chips, cubes).

- Toss two dice. Find the difference.
- Find the number on the chart and place a token on it.
- If no play is possible, lose a turn.
- When each box on the chart is filled, count the tokens.
- Team with the most tokens wins.

| | | | | |
|---|---|---|---|---|
| 0 | 3 | 2 | 1 | 4 |
| 1 | 2 | 5 | 2 | 0 |
| 2 | 1 | 0 | 3 | 1 |
| 0 | 2 | 3 | 1 | 2 |
| 4 | 3 | 2 | 0 | 1 |

**How to Play**

- *Toss a die.*
- *Subtract the number on the die from* ***10.***
- *Fill in the box above the difference.*

| | | | | | |
|---|---|---|---|---|---|
| | | | | | |
| | | | | | |
| | | | | | |
| | | | | | |
| | | | | | |
| **4** | **5** | **6** | **7** | **8** | **9** |

**How to Play**

- Each team tosses a die. Highest number goes first.
- Teams choose a color token (tiles, chips, cubes).

- Toss a die. Subtract the number on the die from **10**. Find the difference on the chart and place a token on it.
- If no play is possible, lose a turn.
- When each box of the chart is filled, count the tokens.
- Team with the most tokens wins.

| | | | | |
|---|---|---|---|---|
| 4 | 6 | 8 | 5 | 7 |
| 8 | 5 | 7 | 9 | 6 |
| 7 | 4 | 6 | 9 | 8 |
| 6 | 9 | 5 | 7 | 4 |
| 4 | 8 | 9 | 5 | 6 |

# 12 Minus Two-Dice-Sum Graph

| 0 | 1 | 2 | 3 | 4 | 5 | 6 | 7 | 8 | 9 | 10 |
|---|---|---|---|---|---|---|---|---|---|----|
|   |   |   |   |   |   |   |   |   |   |    |
|   |   |   |   |   |   |   |   |   |   |    |
|   |   |   |   |   |   |   |   |   |   |    |
|   |   |   |   |   |   |   |   |   |   |    |
|   |   |   |   |   |   |   |   |   |   |    |
|   |   |   |   |   |   |   |   |   |   |    |
|   |   |   |   |   |   |   |   |   |   |    |
|   |   |   |   |   |   |   |   |   |   |    |
|   |   |   |   |   |   |   |   |   |   |    |
|   |   |   |   |   |   |   |   |   |   |    |

# 12 Minus Two-Dice-Sum Chart

**How to Play**

| | | | | |
|---|---|---|---|---|
| 5 | 2 | 7 | 3 | 8 |
| 4 | 6 | 0 | 5 | 6 |
| 8 | 1 | 9 | 3 | 4 |
| 3 | 5 | 10 | 2 | 6 |
| 7 | 6 | 4 | 5 | 7 |

# 15 Minus Two-Dice-Sum Graph

**How to Play**

• Toss two dice. Find the sum.
• Subtract the sum from **15.**
• Fill in the box above the difference.

| 3 | 4 | 5 | 6 | 7 | 8 | 9 | 10 | 11 | 12 | 13 |
|---|---|---|---|---|---|---|----|----|----|----|
|   |   |   |   |   |   |   |    |    |    |    |
|   |   |   |   |   |   |   |    |    |    |    |
|   |   |   |   |   |   |   |    |    |    |    |
|   |   |   |   |   |   |   |    |    |    |    |
|   |   |   |   |   |   |   |    |    |    |    |
|   |   |   |   |   |   |   |    |    |    |    |
|   |   |   |   |   |   |   |    |    |    |    |
|   |   |   |   |   |   |   |    |    |    |    |
|   |   |   |   |   |   |   |    |    |    |    |
|   |   |   |   |   |   |   |    |    |    |    |

# 15 Minus Two-Dice-Sum Chart

- Each team tosses a die. Highest number goes first.
- Teams choose a color token (tiles, chips, cubes).

**How to Play**

- Toss two dice. Find the sum. Subtract the sum from **15.**
- Find the difference on the chart and place a token on the number.
- If no play is possible, lose a turn.
- When each box on the chart is filled, count the tokens.
- Team with the most tokens wins.

| | | | | |
|---|---|---|---|---|
| 7 | 11 | 8 | 6 | 9 |
| 4 | 9 | 5 | 7 | 10 |
| 6 | 8 | 10 | 12 | 6 |
| 3 | 5 | 13 | 4 | 9 |
| 10 | 8 | 7 | 11 | 8 |

# 18 Minus Two-Dice-Sum Graph

**How to Play**

- Toss two dice. Find the sum.
- Subtract the sum from **18.**
- Fill in the box above the difference.

| | | | | | 16 |
|---|---|---|---|---|---|
| | | | | | 15 |
| | | | | | 14 |
| | | | | | 13 |
| | | | | | 12 |
| | | | | | 11 |
| | | | | | 10 |
| | | | | | 9 |
| | | | | | 8 |
| | | | | | 7 |
| | | | | | 6 |

# 18 Minus Two-Dice-Sum Chart

**How to Play**

- Each team tosses a die. Highest number goes first.
- Teams choose a color token (tiles, chips, cubes).

- Toss two dice. Find the sum. Subtract the sum from **18.**
- Find the difference on the chart and place a token on the number.
- If no play is possible, lose a turn.
- When each box on the chart is filled, count the tokens.
- Team with the most tokens wins.

| | | | | |
|---|---|---|---|---|
| **10** | **11** | **8** | **13** | **16** |
| **12** | **14** | **15** | **7** | **10** |
| **6** | **8** | **13** | **12** | **6** |
| **16** | **10** | **9** | **11** | **9** |
| **15** | **11** | **7** | **14** | **12** |

# 100 Minus Two-Dice-Sum Graph

**How to Play**

- Toss two dice. Find the sum.
- Subtract the sum from *100.*
- Fill in the box above the difference.

| 88 | 89 | 90 | 91 | 92 | 93 | 94 | 95 | 96 | 97 | 98 |
|----|----|----|----|----|----|----|----|----|----|----|

# 100 Minus Two-Dice-Sum Chart

How to Play

- Each team tosses a die. Highest number goes first.
- Teams choose a color token (tiles, chips, cubes).

- Toss two dice. Find the sum. Subtract the sum from **100.**
- Find the difference on the chart and place a token on the number.
- If no play is possible, lose a turn.
- When each box on the chart is filled, count the tokens.
- Team with the most tokens wins.

| | | | | |
|---|---|---|---|---|
| 92 | 93 | 90 | 95 | 98 |
| 94 | 96 | 97 | 89 | 92 |
| 88 | 90 | 95 | 94 | 88 |
| 98 | 92 | 91 | 93 | 91 |
| 97 | 93 | 89 | 96 | 94 |

# 85 Minus a Tens Die Graph

- *Toss a die. Each dot equals 10.*
- *Count by tens to find the value of the die.*
- *Subtract the die value from **85.***
- *Fill in the box above the difference.*

| | | | | | |
|---|---|---|---|---|---|
| | | | | | |
| | | | | | |
| | | | | | |
| | | | | | |
| | | | | | |
| **25** | **35** | **45** | **55** | **65** | **75** |

**How to Play**

- Each team tosses a die. Highest number goes first.
- Teams choose a color token (tiles, chips, cubes).

- Toss a die. Each dot equals 10. Count by tens to find the value of the die.
- Subtract the die value from **85.**
- Find the difference on the chart and place a token on it.
- If no play is possible, lose a turn.
- When each box of the chart is filled, count the tokens.
- Team with the most tokens wins.

| 25 | 65 | 35 | 55 | 75 |
|----|----|----|----|----|
| 35 | 55 | 75 | 45 | 65 |
| 75 | 45 | 65 | 25 | 35 |
| 65 | 25 | 55 | 75 | 45 |
| 45 | 35 | 25 | 55 | 65 |

**Dice Activities for Subtraction**

# 100 Minus a Tens Die Graph

**How to Play**

- *Toss a die. Each dot equals 10.*
- *Count by tens to find the value of the die.*
- *Subtract the die value from **100.***
- *Fill in the box above the difference.*

| 40 | 50 | 60 | 70 | 80 | 90 |
|----|----|----|----|----|----|
|    |    |    |    |    |    |
|    |    |    |    |    |    |
|    |    |    |    |    |    |
|    |    |    |    |    |    |
|    |    |    |    |    |    |
|    |    |    |    |    |    |

# 100 Minus a Tens Die Chart

**How to Play**

- Each team tosses a die. Highest number goes first.
- Teams choose a color token (tiles, chips, cubes).

- Toss a die. Each dot equals 10. Count by tens to find the value of the die.
- Subtract the die value from **100.**
- Find the difference on the chart and place a token on it.
- If no play is possible, lose a turn.
- When each box of the chart is filled, count the tokens.
- Team with the most tokens wins.

| 90 | 60 | 80 | 50 | 70 |
|----|----|----|----|----|
| 80 | 50 | 70 | 40 | 60 |
| 70 | 40 | 60 | 90 | 80 |
| 60 | 90 | 50 | 70 | 40 |
| 40 | 80 | 90 | 50 | 60 |

# Create Your Own Die Graph

|  |  |  |  |  |  |
|---|---|---|---|---|---|
|  |  |  |  |  |  |
|  |  |  |  |  |  |
|  |  |  |  |  |  |
|  |  |  |  |  |  |
|  |  |  |  |  |  |
|  |  |  |  |  |  |
|  |  |  |  |  |  |

# Create Your Own Two-Dice Graph

# Create Your Own Die/Two-Dice Chart

|  |  |  |  |  |
|---|---|---|---|---|
|  |  |  |  |  |
|  |  |  |  |  |
|  |  |  |  |  |
|  |  |  |  |  |
|  |  |  |  |  |

# Table Completion Activities

## Contents

# Directions for Table Completion Activities

- Practice computing the difference between two numbers from 0 to 100.
- Recognize number patterns when subtracting from a two-digit number ending in 0.
- Recognize number patterns when subtracting 10 from a two-digit number.
- Recognize number patterns when subtracting multiples of 5 from a two-digit number ending in 0.

Introduce the *Table Completion Charts* activity by demonstrating on an overhead and playing against the class. Two teams with two students on a team are suggested. Playing in teams gives students an opportunity to discuss moves and strategies and provides a check on correct computation.

## Materials
- Chart
- Dice
- Pencil

## How to Play
- Each team tosses a die. The higher number goes first.
- Taking turns, the teams toss a die or dice, circle the die value on the chart, subtract, and then record the solution next to circled number.
- If the number has been played, the team loses a turn.
- If a team records the wrong number, they erase it and lose a turn.
- The first team to complete their chart wins.

## Suggestions
- Before writing a solution on the chart, team members either verbalize the subtraction equation ("11 − 7 = 4") or the difference ("The difference between 11 and 7 is 4.").
- Encourage students to think their way through subtraction as a mental activity. For example, if they are subtracting 20 − 4, ask them to first consider 20 − 5, which is an easier equation to solve. Explore what they would have to do to use the answer from 20 − 5 to solve 20 − 4.
- If students are struggling with subtraction facts, suggest they use the Hundred Chart (page vi) to help them with their calculations.

## Discussion
- Is this a game of luck or skill?

# 6 Minus a Die Table Completion

**How to Play**

- *Each team tosses a die.*
- *Higher number goes first.*

- *Toss a die. Circle the die value on your chart.*
- *Subtract the number tossed from **6** and record the answer in the box next to the die value.*
- *If a box is already filled, lose that turn.*
- *First team to complete their table wins.*

**Team:** _____

| Die Tossed | 6 – |
|:---:|:---:|
| 6 | |
| 5 | |
| 4 | |
| 3 | |
| 2 | |
| 1 | |

**Team:** _____

| Die Tossed | 6 – |
|:---:|:---:|
| 6 | |
| 5 | |
| 4 | |
| 3 | |
| 2 | |
| 1 | |

# 7 Minus a Die Table Completion

**How to Play**

- *Each team tosses a die.*
- *Higher number goes first.*

- *Toss a die. Circle the die value on your chart.*
- *Subtract the number tossed from **7** and record the answer in the box next to the die value.*
- *If a box is already filled, lose that turn.*
- *First team to complete their table wins.*

**Team:** _____

| Die Tossed | 7 – |
|:---:|:---:|
| 6 | |
| 5 | |
| 4 | |
| 3 | |
| 2 | |
| 1 | |

**Team:** _____

| Die Tossed | 7 – |
|:---:|:---:|
| 6 | |
| 5 | |
| 4 | |
| 3 | |
| 2 | |
| 1 | |

# 8 Minus a Die Table Completion

**How to Play**

- Each team tosses a die.
- Higher number goes first.

- Toss a die. Circle the die value on your chart.
- Subtract the number tossed from **8** and record the answer in the box next to the die value.
- If a box is already filled, lose that turn.
- First team to complete their table wins.

**Team:** _____

| Die Tossed | 8 – |
|:---:|:---:|
| 6 | |
| 5 | |
| 4 | |
| 3 | |
| 2 | |
| 1 | |

**Team:** _____

| Die Tossed | 8 – |
|:---:|:---:|
| 6 | |
| 5 | |
| 4 | |
| 3 | |
| 2 | |
| 1 | |

# 9 Minus a Die Table Completion

- Each team tosses a die.
- Higher number goes first.

- Toss a die. Circle the die value on your chart.
- Subtract the number tossed from **9** and record the answer in the box next to the die value.
- If a box is already filled, lose that turn.
- First team to complete their table wins.

**Team:** _____

| Die Tossed | 9 – |
|:---:|:---:|
| 6 | |
| 5 | |
| 4 | |
| 3 | |
| 2 | |
| 1 | |

**Team:** _____

| Die Tossed | 9 – |
|:---:|:---:|
| 6 | |
| 5 | |
| 4 | |
| 3 | |
| 2 | |
| 1 | |

# 10 Minus a Die Table Completion

**How to Play**

- *Each team tosses a die.*
- *Higher number goes first.*

- *Toss a die. Circle the die value on your chart.*
- *Subtract the number tossed from 10 and record the answer in the box next to the die value.*
- *If a box is already filled, lose that turn.*
- *First team to complete their table wins.*

**Team:** _____

| Die Tossed | 10 – |
|:---:|:---:|
| 6 | |
| 5 | |
| 4 | |
| 3 | |
| 2 | |
| 1 | |

**Team:** _____

| Die Tossed | 10 – |
|:---:|:---:|
| 6 | |
| 5 | |
| 4 | |
| 3 | |
| 2 | |
| 1 | |

# 11 Minus a Die Table Completion

**How to Play**

- *Each team tosses a die.*
- *Higher number goes first.*

- *Toss a die. Circle the die value on your chart.*
- *Subtract the number tossed from* **11** *and record the answer in the box next to the die value.*
- *If a box is already filled, lose that turn.*
- *First team to complete their table wins.*

**Team:** _____

| Die Tossed | 11 – |
|:---:|:---:|
| 6 | |
| 5 | |
| 4 | |
| 3 | |
| 2 | |
| 1 | |

**Team:** _____

| Die Tossed | 11 – |
|:---:|:---:|
| 6 | |
| 5 | |
| 4 | |
| 3 | |
| 2 | |
| 1 | |

**How to Play**

- Each team tosses a die.
- Higher number goes first.

- Toss a die. Circle the die value on your chart.
- Subtract the number tossed from **12** and record the answer in the box next to the die value.
- If a box is already filled, lose that turn.
- First team to complete their table wins.

**Team:** _____

| Die Tossed | 12 – |
|:---:|:---:|
| 6 | |
| 5 | |
| 4 | |
| 3 | |
| 2 | |
| 1 | |

**Team:** _____

| Die Tossed | 12 – |
|:---:|:---:|
| 6 | |
| 5 | |
| 4 | |
| 3 | |
| 2 | |
| 1 | |

# 11/12 Minus a Die Table Completion

- *Each team tosses a die.*
- *Higher number goes first.*

- *Toss a die. Circle the die value on your chart.*
- *Subtract the number tossed from* **11** *or* **12** *and record the answer in the box next to the die value.*
- *If a box is already filled, lose that turn.*
- *First team to complete their table wins.*

**Team:** _____

| Die Tossed | 11 – |
|:---:|:---:|
| 6 | |
| 5 | |
| 4 | |
| 3 | |
| 2 | |
| 1 | |

**Team:** _____

| Die Tossed | 12 – |
|:---:|:---:|
| 6 | |
| 5 | |
| 4 | |
| 3 | |
| 2 | |
| 1 | |

# 20 Minus a Die Table Completion

**Team:** _____

| Die Tossed | 20 – |
|:---:|:---:|
| 6 | |
| 5 | |
| 4 | |
| 3 | |
| 2 | |
| 1 | |

**Team:** _____

| Die Tossed | 20 – |
|:---:|:---:|
| 6 | |
| 5 | |
| 4 | |
| 3 | |
| 2 | |
| 1 | |

# 100 Minus a Die Table Completion

**How to Play**

- *Each team tosses a die.*
- *Higher number goes first.*

- *Toss a die. Circle the die value on your chart.*
- *Subtract the number tossed from 100 and record the answer in the box next to the die value.*
- *If a box is already filled, lose that turn.*
- *First team to complete their table wins.*

**Team:** _____

| Die Tossed | 100 – |
|:---:|:---:|
| 6 | |
| 5 | |
| 4 | |
| 3 | |
| 2 | |
| 1 | |

**Team:** _____

| Die Tossed | 100 – |
|:---:|:---:|
| 6 | |
| 5 | |
| 4 | |
| 3 | |
| 2 | |
| 1 | |

# 60/80 Minus a Die Table Completion

- Each team tosses a die.
- Higher number goes first.

- Toss a die. Circle the die value on your chart.
- Subtract the number tossed from **60** or **80** and record the answer in the box next to the die value.
- If a box is already filled, lose that turn.
- First team to complete their table wins.

**Team:** _____

| Die Tossed | 60 – |
|:---:|:---:|
| 6 | |
| 5 | |
| 4 | |
| 3 | |
| 2 | |
| 1 | |

**Team:** _____

| Die Tossed | 80 – |
|:---:|:---:|
| 6 | |
| 5 | |
| 4 | |
| 3 | |
| 2 | |
| 1 | |

# 20 Minus Two-Dice-Sum Table Completion

- Toss 2 dice. Find the sum. Circle the sum on your chart.
- Subtract the sum from **20.** Record the answer next to the sum in the table.
- If the sum has already been tossed, lose a turn.
- First team to complete their table wins.

Team: _____

Team: _____

| Sum | 20 – |
| --- | --- |
| 12 | |
| 11 | |
| 10 | |
| 9 | |
| 8 | |
| 7 | |
| 6 | |
| 5 | |
| 4 | |
| 3 | |
| 2 | |

| Sum | 20 – |
| --- | --- |
| 12 | |
| 11 | |
| 10 | |
| 9 | |
| 8 | |
| 7 | |
| 6 | |
| 5 | |
| 4 | |
| 3 | |
| 2 | |

# 50/30 Minus Two-Dice-Sum Table Completion

**How to Play**

- Each team tosses a die.
- Higher number goes first.

- Toss 2 dice. Find the sum. Circle the sum on your chart.
- Subtract the sum from **50** or **30.** Record the answer next to the sum in the table.
- If the sum has already been tossed, lose a turn.
- First team to complete their table wins.

**Team:** _____

**Team:** _____

| Sum | 50 – |
|:---:|:---:|
| 12 | |
| 11 | |
| 10 | |
| 9 | |
| 8 | |
| 7 | |
| 6 | |
| 5 | |
| 4 | |
| 3 | |
| 2 | |

| Sum | 30 – |
|:---:|:---:|
| 12 | |
| 11 | |
| 10 | |
| 9 | |
| 8 | |
| 7 | |
| 6 | |
| 5 | |
| 4 | |
| 3 | |
| 2 | |

# 74/64 Minus a Tens Die Table Completion

**How to Play**

- Each team tosses a die.
- Higher number goes first.

- Toss a die. Each dot equals 10. Count by tens to find the value of the die.
- Circle the die value on your chart.
- Subtract the die value from either **74** or **64** and record the answer in the box next to the die value.
- If a box is already filled, lose that turn.
- First team to complete their table wins.

**Team:** _____

**Team:** _____

| Die Tossed | 74 – |
| --- | --- |
| 50 | |
| 20 | |
| 40 | |
| 60 | |
| 10 | |
| 30 | |

| Die Tossed | 64 – |
| --- | --- |
| 20 | |
| 40 | |
| 60 | |
| 10 | |
| 30 | |
| 50 | |

# 90/80 Minus a Tens Die Table Completion

**How to Play**

- *Each team tosses a die.*
- *Higher number goes first.*

- *Toss a die. Each dot equals 10. Count by tens to find the value of the die.*
- *Circle the die value on your chart.*
- *Subtract the die value from either **90** or **80** and record the answer in the box next to the die value.*
- *If a box is already filled, lose that turn.*
- *First team to complete their table wins.*

**Team:** _____

| Die Tossed | 90 – |
|:---:|:---:|
| 50 | |
| 20 | |
| 40 | |
| 60 | |
| 10 | |
| 30 | |

**Team:** _____

| Die Tossed | 80 – |
|:---:|:---:|
| 20 | |
| 40 | |
| 60 | |
| 10 | |
| 30 | |
| 50 | |

# 50 Minus a Fives Die Table Completion

**How to Play**

- *Each team tosses a die.*
- *Higher number goes first.*

- *Toss a die. Each dot equals 5. Count by fives to find the value of the die.*
- *Circle the die value on your chart.*
- *Subtract the die value from* **50** *and record the answer in the box next to the die value.*
- *If a box is already filled, lose that turn.*
- *First team to complete their table wins.*

**Team:** _____

| Die Tossed | 50 – |
|:---:|:---:|
| 5 | |
| 20 | |
| 15 | |
| 30 | |
| 25 | |
| 10 | |

**Team:** _____

| Die Tossed | 50 – |
|:---:|:---:|
| 20 | |
| 15 | |
| 5 | |
| 10 | |
| 30 | |
| 25 | |

# Create Your Own One-Die
# Table Completion Chart

Team: _____

Team: _____

| Die Tossed | |
|:---:|:---:|
| **6** | |
| **5** | |
| **4** | |
| **3** | |
| **2** | |
| **1** | |

| Die Tossed | |
|:---:|:---:|
| **6** | |
| **5** | |
| **4** | |
| **3** | |
| **2** | |
| **1** | |

Team: _____

| Sum | |
|:---:|:---:|
| 12 | |
| 11 | |
| 10 | |
| 9 | |
| 8 | |
| 7 | |
| 6 | |
| 5 | |
| 4 | |
| 3 | |
| 2 | |

Team: _____

| Sum | |
|:---:|:---:|
| 12 | |
| 11 | |
| 10 | |
| 9 | |
| 8 | |
| 7 | |
| 6 | |
| 5 | |
| 4 | |
| 3 | |
| 2 | |

# Rounds Activities

## Contents

# Directions for Rounds Activities

- Develop a sense of number and number patterns when subtracting numbers 1 through 85.
- Practice subtracting numbers 1 through 6 from numbers ranging from 7 to 61.
- Recognize number patterns when subtracting a multiple of 5 or 10 from a two-digit number ending in 5.

The **Rounds** activities help students to develop an awareness of number patterns. Introduce the **Rounds** activity by demonstrating on an overhead. Two teams with two students on a team are suggested.

## Materials

- Chart
- Dice
- Tokens (tiles, chips, cubes)

## How to Play

### Round 1

- Taking turns, teams toss 1 or 2 dice, depending on the activity.
- The team performs the required computation and places a token on the answer in the first row of their chart.
- If the number has a token on it, the team loses that turn.
- The first team to place tokens on all six numbers in the row wins that round, and play moves to the next round.

### Rounds 2 and 3

- Directions are the same as for Round 1.
- The team winning two out of three rounds wins the game.

## Suggestions

- Encourage students to think their way through subtraction as a mental activity. For example, if they are subtracting $15 - 4$, ask them to first consider $15 - 5$, which is an easier equation to solve. Explore what they would have to do to use the answer from $15 - 5$ to solve $15 - 4$.
- If students are struggling with subtraction facts, suggest they use the Hundred Chart (page vi) to help them with their calculations.

## Variation

- The team with the most tokens on their chart after three rounds wins the game.
- A team only moves on to the next round when each number in the row has a token on it. The first team to fill their chart wins.

## Discussion

- Is this a game of luck or skill?
- How might it be possible for a team to have the most tokens on their chart yet not win two out of threes rounds?
- How does this activity help you learn subtraction patterns?

# 6, 7, 8 Minus a Die Rounds

**How to Play**

- *Each team tosses a die.*
- *Higher number goes first.*
- *Each team gets a chart.*

**Round 1**

- Toss a die. Subtract the number on the die from **6**. Place a token on the difference.
- If the difference has a token on it, lose a turn. First team to place tokens on all six differences wins Round 1.

**Round 2**

- Toss a die. Subtract the number on the die from **7**. Place a token on the difference. First team to place tokens on all six differences wins Round 2.

**Round 3**

- Toss a die. Subtract the number on the die from **8**. Place a token on the difference. First team to place tokens on all six differences wins Round 3.
- Team winning 2 out of 3 rounds is the winner.

| Round 1 | 6 | 0 | 1 | 2 | 3 | 4 | 5 |
|---|---|---|---|---|---|---|---|
| Round 2 | 7 | 1 | 2 | 3 | 4 | 5 | 6 |
| Round 3 | 8 | 2 | 3 | 4 | 5 | 6 | 7 |

# 9, 10, 11 Minus a Die Rounds

- Each team tosses a die.
- Higher number goes first.
- Each team gets a chart.

**Round 1**

- Toss a die. Subtract the number on the die from **9.** Place a token on the difference.
- If the difference has a token on it, lose a turn. First team to place tokens on all six differences wins Round 1.

**Round 2**

- Toss a die. Subtract the number on the die from **10.** Place a token on the difference. First team to place tokens on all six differences wins Round 2.

**Round 3**

- Toss a die. Subtract the number on the die from **11.** Place a token on the difference. First team to place tokens on all six differences wins Round 3.
- Team winning 2 out of 3 rounds is the winner.

| Round 1 | | | | | | |
|---|---|---|---|---|---|---|
| **9** | 3 | 4 | 5 | 6 | 7 | 8 |

| Round 2 | | | | | | |
|---|---|---|---|---|---|---|
| **10** | 4 | 5 | 6 | 7 | 8 | 9 |

| Round 3 | | | | | | |
|---|---|---|---|---|---|---|
| **11** | 5 | 6 | 7 | 8 | 9 | 10 |

# 12, 13, 14 Minus a Die Rounds

**How to Play**

- Each team tosses a die.
- Higher number goes first.
- Each team gets a chart.

**Round 1**

- Toss a die. Subtract the number on the die from **12.** Place a token on the difference.
- If the difference has a token on it, lose a turn. First team to place tokens on all six differences wins Round 1.

**Round 2**

- Toss a die. Subtract the number on the die from **13.** Place a token on the difference. First team to place tokens on all six differences wins Round 2.

**Round 3**

- Toss a die. Subtract the number on the die from **14.** Place a token on the difference. First team to place tokens on all six differences wins Round 3.
- Team winning 2 out of 3 rounds is the winner.

| Round 1 | 12 | 6 | 7 | 8 | 9 | 10 | 11 |
| --- | --- | --- | --- | --- | --- | --- | --- |
| Round 2 | 13 | 7 | 8 | 9 | 10 | 11 | 12 |
| Round 3 | 14 | 8 | 9 | 10 | 11 | 12 | 13 |

# 15, 16, 17 Minus a Die Rounds

**How to Play**

- Each team tosses a die.
- Higher number goes first.
- Each team gets a chart.

**Round 1**

- Toss a die. Subtract the number on the die from **15**. Place a token on the difference.
- If the difference has a token on it, lose a turn. First team to place tokens on all six differences wins Round 1.

**Round 2**

- Toss a die. Subtract the number on the die from **16**. Place a token on the difference. First team to place tokens on all six differences wins Round 2.

**Round 3**

- Toss a die. Subtract the number on the die from **17**. Place a token on the difference. First team to place tokens on all six differences wins Round 3.
- Team winning 2 out of 3 rounds is the winner.

| Round 1 | 15 | | 9 | 10 | 11 | 12 | 13 | 14 |
| Round 2 | 16 | | 10 | 11 | 12 | 13 | 14 | 15 |
| Round 3 | 17 | | 11 | 12 | 13 | 14 | 15 | 16 |

# 18, 19, 20 Minus a Die Rounds

**How to Play**

- Each team tosses a die.
- Higher number goes first.
- Each team gets a chart.

**Round 1**
- Toss a die. Subtract the number on the die from **18**. Place a token on the difference.
- If the difference has a token on it, lose a turn. First team to place tokens on all six differences wins Round 1.

**Round 2**
- Toss a die. Subtract the number on the die from **19**. Place a token on the difference. First team to place tokens on all six differences wins Round 2.

**Round 3**
- Toss a die. Subtract the number on the die from **20**. Place a token on the difference. First team to place tokens on all six differences wins Round 3.
- Team winning 2 out of 3 rounds is the winner.

| Round 1 | 18 | 12 | 13 | 14 | 15 | 16 | 17 |
|---------|----|----|----|----|----|----|----|

| Round 2 | 19 | 13 | 14 | 15 | 16 | 17 | 18 |
|---------|----|----|----|----|----|----|----|

| Round 3 | 20 | 14 | 15 | 16 | 17 | 18 | 19 |
|---------|----|----|----|----|----|----|----|

# 41, 51, 61 Minus a Die Rounds

- Each team tosses a die.
- Higher number goes first.
- Each team gets a chart.

**Round 1**
- Toss a die. Subtract the number on the die from **41**. Place a token on the difference.
- If the difference has a token on it, lose a turn. First team to place tokens on all six differences wins Round 1.

**Round 2**
- Toss a die. Subtract the number on the die from **51**. Place a token on the difference. First team to place tokens on all six differences wins Round 2.

**Round 3**
- Toss a die. Subtract the number on the die from **61**. Place a token on the difference. First team to place tokens on all six differences wins Round 3.
- Team winning 2 out of 3 rounds is the winner.

| Round 1 | 41 | 36 | 38 | 39 | 35 | 40 | 37 |
| --- | --- | --- | --- | --- | --- | --- | --- |
| Round 2 | 51 | 48 | 47 | 45 | 50 | 49 | 46 |
| Round 3 | 61 | 55 | 59 | 60 | 57 | 56 | 58 |

# 65, 75, 85 Minus a Tens Die Rounds

### How to Play

- Each team tosses a die.
- Higher number goes first.
- Each team gets a chart.

**Round 1**

- Toss a die. Each dot equals 10. Count by tens to find the value of the die.
- Subtract the die value from **65.** Place a token on the difference.
- If the difference has a token on it, lose a turn. First team to place tokens on all six differences wins Round 1.

**Round 2**

- Toss a die and count by tens to compute the die value. Subtract the die value from **75.** Place a token on the difference. First team to place tokens on all six differences wins Round 2.

**Round 3**

- Toss a die and count by tens to compute the die value. Subtract the die value from **85.** Place a token on the difference. First team to place tokens on all six differences wins Round 3.
- Team winning 2 out of 3 rounds is the winner.

| Round 1 | 65 | 35 | 15 | 55 | 25 | 5 | 45 |
|---------|----|----|----|----|----|----|----|
| Round 2 | 75 | 65 | 55 | 35 | 15 | 45 | 25 |
| Round 3 | 85 | 25 | 65 | 45 | 75 | 35 | 55 |

**Dice Activities for Subtraction**

# 35, 45, 55 Minus a Fives Die Rounds

| | How to Play |
|---|---|
| • Each team tosses a die. | |
| • Higher number goes first. | |
| • Each team gets a chart. | |

**Round 1**
- Toss a die. Each dot equals 5. Count by fives to find the value of the die.
- Subtract the die value from **35.** Place a token on the difference.
- If the difference has a token on it, lose a turn. First team to place tokens on all six differences wins Round 1.

**Round 2**
- Toss a die and count by fives to compute the die value. Subtract the die value from **45.** Place a token on the difference. First team to place tokens on all six differences wins Round 2.

**Round 3**
- Toss a die and count by fives to compute the die value. Subtract the die value from **55.** Place a token on the difference. First team to place tokens on all six differences wins Round 3.
- Team winning 2 out of 3 rounds is the winner.

| Round 1 | 35 | 20 | 10 | 30 | 25 | 5 | 15 |
|---|---|---|---|---|---|---|---|
| Round 2 | 45 | 25 | 40 | 15 | 35 | 30 | 20 |
| Round 3 | 55 | 40 | 25 | 35 | 30 | 50 | 45 |

# Create Your Own Rounds Chart

| Round 1 | Round 2 | Round 3 |
|---------|---------|---------|
|         |         |         |
|         |         |         |
|         |         |         |
|         |         |         |
|         |         |         |
|         |         |         |
|         |         |         |

# Pattern Toss and Pattern Round Activities

# Directions for Pattern Toss and Pattern Rounds Activities

## Objectives

- Recognize number patterns when subtracting numbers 1 through 6 from a number with 7 in the ones place.
- Recognize number patterns when subtracting the numbers 1 through 6 from a multiple of 10.
- Recognize number patterns when subtracting a multiple of 10 from a multiple of 10.
- Recognize number patterns when subtracting a multiple of 10 from a two-digit number.
- Recognize number patterns when subtracting a multiple of 5 from a multiple of 10.

Introduce the **Pattern Toss** and **Pattern Rounds** activities by demonstrating on an overhead and playing against the class. Two teams with two students on a team are suggested. Playing as teams gives students an opportunity to discuss moves and strategies and provides a check on correct computation.

## Materials

- Chart
- Dice
- Pencil

## How to Play

### Pattern Toss Activities

- Taking turns, teams toss a die or dice and record the solution on one of their two charts.
- If the number has been played on both of their charts, the team loses a turn.
- If a team records the wrong number, they erase it and lose a turn.
- The first team to complete both their charts wins.

### Pattern Round Activities

- Taking turns, the teams toss 1 or 2 dice depending on the activity.

- Starting with Round 1, the teams find the required difference and place a token on it in the first row of their chart.
- If the difference has a token on it, the team loses a turn.
- The first team to place tokens on all six differences wins that round.
- The teams move on to the next round.
- The team winning 2 out of 3 rounds wins.

## Suggestions

- Before placing a token on the chart, team members either verbalize the subtraction equation (17 − 7 = 10) or the difference ("The difference between 17 and 7 is 10.").

## Discussion

- What is the same about the solutions in each row?
- How did the number patterns help you find the solutions?
- How did playing the Pattern Toss activities first help you to find the solutions in the Rounds activities?

# 7, 17, 27, 37 Minus a Die Pattern Toss

**How to Play**

- Toss a die. Circle the die value on either of your team's charts.
- Subtract the die value from the number at the top of the chart.
- Record the difference in the box next to the die value.
- If the number has already been tossed, lose a turn.
- First team to complete both their charts wins.

| Die Tossed | 37– |
|---|---|
| 6 | |
| 5 | |
| 4 | |
| 3 | |
| 2 | |
| 1 | |

| Die Tossed | 27– |
|---|---|
| 6 | |
| 5 | |
| 4 | |
| 3 | |
| 2 | |
| 1 | |

| Die Tossed | 17– |
|---|---|
| 6 | |
| 5 | |
| 4 | |
| 3 | |
| 2 | |
| 1 | |

| Die Tossed | 7– |
|---|---|
| 6 | |
| 5 | |
| 4 | |
| 3 | |
| 2 | |
| 1 | |

# 7, 17, 27 Minus a Die Pattern Rounds

**How to Play**

- Each team tosses a die.
- Higher number goes first.
- Each team gets a chart.

**Round 1**

- Toss a die. Subtract the number on the die from **7.** Place a token on the difference.
- If the difference has a token on it, lose a turn. First team to place tokens on all six differences wins Round 1.

**Round 2**

- Toss a die. Subtract the number on the die from **17.** Place a token on the difference. First team to place tokens on all six differences wins Round 2.

**Round 3**

- Toss a die. Subtract the number on the die from **27.** Place a token on the difference. First team to place tokens on all six differences wins Round 3.
- Team winning 2 out of 3 rounds is the winner.

| Round 1 | 7 | 2 | 6 | 4 | 1 | 5 | 3 |
|---|---|---|---|---|---|---|---|
| Round 2 | 17 | 14 | 12 | 16 | 13 | 15 | 11 |
| Round 3 | 27 | 24 | 22 | 23 | 26 | 21 | 25 |

# 10, 20, 30, 40 Minus a Die Pattern Toss

## How to Play

- Toss a die. Circle the die value on either of your team's charts.
- Subtract the die value from the number at the top of the chart.
- Record the difference in the box next to the die value.
- If the number has already been tossed, lose a turn.
- First team to complete both their charts wins.

- Each team tosses a die.
- Higher number goes first.
- Lower number chooses two charts.

| Die tossed | 30 − |
|:---:|:---:|
| 6 | |
| 5 | |
| 4 | |
| 3 | |
| 2 | |
| 1 | |

| Die tossed | 20 − |
|:---:|:---:|
| 6 | |
| 5 | |
| 4 | |
| 3 | |
| 2 | |
| 1 | |

| Die tossed | 40 − |
|:---:|:---:|
| 6 | |
| 5 | |
| 4 | |
| 3 | |
| 2 | |
| 1 | |

| Die tossed | 10 − |
|:---:|:---:|
| 6 | |
| 5 | |
| 4 | |
| 3 | |
| 2 | |
| 1 | |

# 10, 20, 30 Minus a Die Pattern Rounds

- Each team tosses a die.
- Higher number goes first.
- Each team gets a chart.

**Round 1**

- Toss a die. Subtract the number on the die from **10**. Place a token on the difference.
- If the difference has a token on it, lose a turn. First team to place tokens on all six differences wins Round 1.

**Round 2**

- Toss a die. Subtract the number on the die from **20**. Place a token on the difference. First team to place tokens on all six differences wins Round 2.

**Round 3**

- Toss a die. Subtract the number on the die from **30**. Place a token on the difference. First team to place tokens on all six differences wins Round 3.
- Team winning 2 out of 3 rounds is the winner.

| Round 1 | 10 | 7 | 6 | 4 | 9 | 5 | 8 |
|---------|----|---|---|---|---|---|---|
| Round 2 | 20 | 16 | 14 | 19 | 17 | 18 | 15 |
| Round 3 | 30 | 24 | 25 | 26 | 28 | 27 | 29 |

# 100, 90, 80, 70 Minus a Tens Die Pattern Toss

**How to Play**

- Each team tosses a die.
- Higher number goes first.
- Lower number chooses two charts.

- Toss a die. Each dot equals 10. Count by tens to find the value of the die.
- Circle the die value on either of your team's charts.
- Subtract the die value from the number at the top of the chart and record the difference in the box next to the die value.
- If the number has already been tossed, lose a turn.
- First team to complete both their charts wins.

| Die Tossed | 90 – |
|---|---|
| 60 | |
| 50 | |
| 40 | |
| 30 | |
| 20 | |
| 10 | |

| Die Tossed | 70 – |
|---|---|
| 60 | |
| 50 | |
| 40 | |
| 30 | |
| 20 | |
| 10 | |

| Die Tossed | 80 – |
|---|---|
| 60 | |
| 50 | |
| 40 | |
| 30 | |
| 20 | |
| 10 | |

| Die Tossed | 100 – |
|---|---|
| 60 | |
| 50 | |
| 40 | |
| 30 | |
| 20 | |
| 10 | |

# 100, 90, 80 Minus a Tens Die Pattern Rounds

- Each team tosses a die.
- Higher number goes first.
- Each team gets a chart.

### Round 1
- Toss a die. Each dot equals 10. Count by tens to find the value of the die.
- Subtract the die value from **100.** Place a token on the difference.
- If the difference has a token on it, lose a turn.
- First team to place tokens on all six differences wins Round 1.

### Round 2
- Toss a die and count by tens to compute the die value. Subtract the die value from **90.** Place a token on the difference. First team to place tokens on all six differences wins Round 2.

### Round 3
- Toss a die and count by tens to compute the die value. Subtract the die value from **80.** Place a token on the difference. First team to place tokens on all six differences wins Round 3.

| Round 1 | 100 | 80 | 40 | 60 | 90 | 50 | 70 |
| Round 2 | 90 | 50 | 70 | 30 | 60 | 40 | 80 |
| Round 3 | 80 | 40 | 60 | 50 | 20 | 70 | 30 |

# 98, 88, 78, 68 Minus a Tens Die Pattern Toss

**How to Play**

- Toss a die. Each dot equals 10. Count by tens to find the value of the die.
- Circle the die value on either of your team's charts.
- Subtract the die value from the number at the top of the chart and record the difference in the box next to the die value.
- If the number has already been tossed, lose a turn.
- First team to complete both their charts wins.

- Each team tosses a die.
- Higher number goes first.
- Lower number chooses two charts.

| Die Tossed | 78 – |
|---|---|
| 60 | |
| 50 | |
| 40 | |
| 30 | |
| 20 | |
| 10 | |

| Die Tossed | 98 – |
|---|---|
| 60 | |
| 50 | |
| 40 | |
| 30 | |
| 20 | |
| 10 | |

| Die Tossed | 68 – |
|---|---|
| 60 | |
| 50 | |
| 40 | |
| 30 | |
| 20 | |
| 10 | |

| Die Tossed | 88 – |
|---|---|
| 60 | |
| 50 | |
| 40 | |
| 30 | |
| 20 | |
| 10 | |

# 98, 88, 78 Minus a Tens Die Pattern Rounds

- Each team tosses a die.
- Higher number goes first.
- Each team gets a chart.

**Round 1**

- Toss a die. Each dot equals 10. Count by tens to find the value of the die.
- Subtract the die value from **98.** Place a token on the difference.
- If the difference has a token on it, lose a turn.
- First team to place tokens on all six differences wins Round 1.

**Round 2**

- Toss a die and count by tens to compute the die value. Subtract the die value from **88.** Place a token on the difference. First team to place tokens on all six differences wins Round 2..

**Round 3**

- Toss a die and count by tens to compute the die value. Subtract the die value from **78.** Place a token on the difference. First team to place tokens on all six differences wins Round 3.

| Round 1 | 98 | 88 | 48 | 68 | 38 | 58 | 78 |
| --- | --- | --- | --- | --- | --- | --- | --- |
| Round 2 | 88 | 58 | 78 | 38 | 68 | 48 | 28 |
| Round 3 | 78 | 48 | 68 | 58 | 28 | 18 | 38 |

# 30, 40, 50, 60 Minus a Fives Die Pattern Toss

**How to Play**

- Each team tosses a die.
- Higher number goes first.
- Lower number chooses two charts.

- Toss a die. Each dot equals 5. Count by fives to find the value of the die.
- Circle the die value on either of your team's charts.
- Subtract the die value from the number at the top of the chart and record the difference in the box next to the die value.
- If the number has already been tossed, lose a turn.
- First team to complete both their charts wins.

| Die Tossed | 30 – |
|---|---|
| 30 | |
| 25 | |
| 20 | |
| 15 | |
| 10 | |
| 5 | |

| Die Tossed | 40 – |
|---|---|
| 30 | |
| 25 | |
| 20 | |
| 15 | |
| 10 | |
| 5 | |

| Die Tossed | 50 – |
|---|---|
| 30 | |
| 25 | |
| 20 | |
| 15 | |
| 10 | |
| 5 | |

| Die Tossed | 60 – |
|---|---|
| 30 | |
| 25 | |
| 20 | |
| 15 | |
| 10 | |
| 5 | |

# 30, 40, 50 Minus a Fives Die Pattern Rounds

**How to Play**

- Each team tosses a die.
- Higher number goes first.
- Each team gets a chart.

### Round 1

- Toss a die. Each dot equals 5. Count by fives to find the value of the die.
- Subtract the die value from **30.** Place a token on the difference.
- If the difference has a token on it, lose a turn.
- First team to place tokens on all six differences wins Round 1.

### Round 2

- Toss a die and count by tens to compute the die value. Subtract the die value from **40.** Place a token on the difference. First team to place tokens on all six differences wins Round 2.

### Round 3

- Toss a die and count by tens to compute the die value. Subtract the die value from **50.** Place a token on the difference. First team to place tokens on all six differences wins Round 3.

| Round 1 | 30 | 20 | 0 | 10 | 25 | 5 | 15 |
| Round 2 | 40 | 25 | 10 | 35 | 15 | 30 | 20 |
| Round 3 | 50 | 40 | 20 | 35 | 30 | 25 | 45 |

# Create Your Own Pattern Toss

**How to Play**

- Each team tosses a die.
- Higher number goes first.
- Lower number chooses two charts.

- Toss a die. Each dot equals _____. Count by _____ to find the value of the die.
- Circle the die value on either of your team's charts.
- Subtract the die value from the number at the top of the chart and record the difference in the box next to the die value.
- If the number has already been tossed, lose a turn.
- First team to complete both their charts wins.

| | | | | | | |
|---|---|---|---|---|---|---|
| **Die Tossed** | | | | | | |

| | | | | | | |
|---|---|---|---|---|---|---|
| **Die Tossed** | | | | | | |

| | | | | | | |
|---|---|---|---|---|---|---|
| **Die Tossed** | | | | | | |

| | | | | | | |
|---|---|---|---|---|---|---|
| **Die Tossed** | | | | | | |

# Create Your Own Pattern Rounds

- Each team tosses a die.
- Higher number goes first.
- Each team gets a chart.

**Round 1**

- Toss a die. Each dot equals _____ Count by _____ to find the value of the die.
- Subtract the die value from _____. Place a token on the difference.
- If the difference has a token on it, lose a turn.
- First team to place tokens on all six differences wins Round 1.

**Round 2**

- Toss a die and count by _____ to compute the die value. Subtract the die value from _____. Place a token on the difference. First team to place tokens on all six differences wins Round 2.

**Round 3**

- Toss a die and count by _____ to compute the die value. Subtract the die value from _____. Place a token on the difference. First team to place tokens on all six differences wins Round 3.

**Round 1**

| | | | | | | |
|---|---|---|---|---|---|---|
| | | | | | | |

**Round 2**

| | | | | | | |
|---|---|---|---|---|---|---|
| | | | | | | |

**Round 3**

| | | | | | | |
|---|---|---|---|---|---|---|
| | | | | | | |

# Differences Activities

# Directions for Differences Activities

- Recognize the difference between numbers 0 to 6.
- Recognize the difference between multiples of 10 and numbers 0, 10, 20, 30, 40, 50, and 60.
- Recognize the difference between multiples of 5 and numbers 0, 5, 10, 15, 20, 25, and 30.
- Develop a sense of number patterns when subtracting multiples of 5 and 10 from a two-digit number ending in 0 or 5.

Introduce each **Differences** activity by demonstrating on an overhead. Two teams with two students on a team are suggested.

## Materials
- Chart for each team
- 6 dice for each team
- Tokens (tiles, chips, cubes)

## How to Play

### Differences 0, 1, 2, 3, 4, 5
- Taking turns, each team tosses their 6 dice. The team removes pairs of dice with a difference of 0, 1, 2, 3, 4, or 5, placing each dice pair in the box on the chart that shows the difference.
- After all possible dice pairs have been placed on the chart, the team replaces each pair with a token.
- The first team to fill their chart is the winner.

### Differences 0, 10, 20, 30, 40, 50
- Taking turns, each team tosses their 6 dice. For this activity, each dot on a die equals 10. The team players count by tens to find the value of each die.
- The team selects pairs of dice with a difference of 0, 10, 20, 30, 40, or 50, placing each dice pair in the box on the chart that shows the difference.

- After all possible dice pairs have been placed on the chart, the team replaces each pair with a token.
- The first team to fill their chart is the winner.

### Differences 0, 5, 10, 15, 20, 25
- Taking turns, each team tosses their 6 dice. For this activity, each dot on a die equals 5. The team players count by fives to find the value of each die.
- The team selects pairs of dice with a difference of 0, 5, 10, 15, 20, or 25, placing each dice pair in the box on the chart that shows the difference.
- After all possible dice pairs have been placed on the chart, the team replaces each pair with a token.
- The first team to fill their chart is the winner.

## Suggestions
- Encourage students to think their way through subtraction as a mental activity. If they are subtracting 50 − 30, have them first consider 5 − 3, which is an easier equation to solve. Explore what they would have to do to use the answer from 5 − 3 to solve 50 − 30.

- If students are struggling with subtraction facts, suggest they use the Hundred Chart (page vi) to help them with their computation.

## Variations

- The team with the most tokens on their chart after 5 tosses wins.
- Teams must first select two dice with a difference of 0, then differences of 2, 3, 4, and 5 in order. A team moves on to the next row only when each number in the row has a token on it. The first team to fill their chart, or the team with the most tokens after 10 tosses, wins.
- The teams toss 8, 10, or 12 dice instead of six.
- The teams toss fewer dice—2 or 4.

## Discussion

- Is this a game of luck or skill?
- What differences are the most difficult to toss? The least difficult? How might this influence your strategy for pairing dice?
- How does this activity help you learn subtraction facts?

## 12-Dice Difference High and 12 Dice Difference Low

### Materials

- 6 green dice and 6 red dice
- Score sheet
- Pencil

### How to Play

- Each team tosses a die. The higher number goes first for Toss 1. It is important that teams alternate going first for Tosses 2 through 4.
- A player tosses all 12 dice—6 green dice and 6 red dice.

## *12-Dice High*

- Teams take turns pairing a red die and a green die from the group of 12 dice, aiming to get the *largest* difference between the two dice.
- When all 12 dice have been paired, the teams record the sum of their differences on the chart.
- After four rounds, the teams tally their scores. The team with the highest score wins.

## *12-Dice Low*

- Teams take turns pairing a red die and a green die from the group of 12 dice, aiming to get the *smallest* difference between the two dice.
- When all 12 dice have been paired, the teams record the sum of their differences on the chart.
- After four rounds, the teams tally their scores. The team with the lowest score wins.

## Suggestions

- Before the teams tally their results, they predict which team will win.

## Variations

- Add more dice to the activity.
- Use fewer dice.

## Discussion

- Is this more a game of luck or skill?
- Is there an advantage to going first?
- Would adding more dice to the activity influence the outcome? (How many dice do you need to make this a fair game?)
- Would adding a fifth toss to the activity influence the outcome? Would it be a fair game?
- Would adding a third team to the activity influence the outcome?
- Would it be a fair game?

# Differences 0, 1, 2, 3, 4, 5

- *Each team tosses a die.*
- *Higher number goes first.*

**How to Play**

- *Taking turns, toss 6 dice and select pairs of dice with a difference of **0, 1, 2, 3, 4,** or **5.***
- *Place each dice pair in a box on the chart that shows the difference.*
- *After all possible pairs have been placed, replace each dice pair with a token.*
- *First team to place a token in every box of their chart wins.*

| Difference 0 | Difference 0 | Difference 0 |
|:---:|:---:|:---:|
| **Difference 1** | **Difference 1** | **Difference 1** |
| **Difference 2** | **Difference 2** | **Difference 2** |
| **Difference 3** | **Difference 3** | **Difference 3** |
| **Difference 4** | **Difference 4** | **Difference 4** |
| **Difference 5** | **Difference 5** | **Difference 5** |

# Differences 0, 10, 20, 30, 40, 50

- Each team tosses a die.
- Higher number goes first.

**How to Play**

- Toss 6 dice. Each dot on a die equals 10. Count by tens to find the value of each die.
- Select pairs of dice with a difference of **0, 10, 20, 30, 40,** or **50.**
- Place each dice pair in a box on the chart that shows the difference.
- After all possible pairs have been placed, replace each dice pair with a token.
- First team to place tokens in every box of their chart wins.

| Difference **0** | Difference **0** | Difference **0** |
|---|---|---|
| Difference **10** | Difference **10** | Difference **10** |
| Difference **20** | Difference **20** | Difference **20** |
| Difference **30** | Difference **30** | Difference **30** |
| Difference **40** | Difference **40** | Difference **40** |
| Difference **50** | Difference **50** | Difference **50** |

# Differences 0, 5, 10, 15, 20, 25

- Each team tosses a die.
- Higher number goes first.

**How to Play**

- Toss 6 dice. Each dot on a die equals 5. Count by fives to find the value of each die.
- Select pairs of dice with a difference of **0, 5, 10, 15, 20,** or **25.**
- Place each dice pair in a box on the chart that shows the difference.
- After all possible pairs have been placed, replace each dice pair with a token.
- First team to place tokens in every box of their chart wins.

| Difference 0 | Difference 0 | Difference 0 |
|:---:|:---:|:---:|
| **Difference 5** | **Difference 5** | **Difference 5** |
| **Difference 10** | **Difference 10** | **Difference 10** |
| **Difference 15** | **Difference 15** | **Difference 15** |
| **Difference 20** | **Difference 20** | **Difference 20** |
| **Difference 25** | **Difference 25** | **Difference 25** |

- Each team tosses a die. Higher number goes first for Toss 1.

- Teams take turns going first for Tosses 2 through 4.

- One player tosses all 12 dice—6 green dice and 6 red dice.

- Taking turns, teams remove a red die and a green die from the group of 12 dice, aiming for the **largest** difference between a red die and a green die.

- For each toss, when all 12 dice have been removed, tally and record the sum of the differences on the chart.

- After 4 rounds, teams total their scores. Team with the **highest** score wins.

| Toss | Team A | Team B |
|------|--------|--------|
| 1 | | |
| 2 | | |
| 3 | | |
| 4 | | |
| Total | | |

| Toss | Team A | Team B |
|------|--------|--------|
| 1 | | |
| 2 | | |
| 3 | | |
| 4 | | |
| Total | | |

# 12-Dice Difference Low

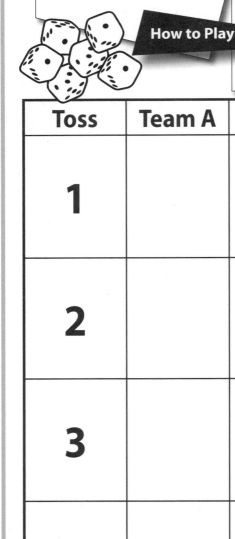
| Toss | Team A | Team B |
|------|--------|--------|
| 1 | | |
| 2 | | |
| 3 | | |
| 4 | | |
| Total | | |

| Toss | Team A | Team B |
|------|--------|--------|
| 1 | | |
| 2 | | |
| 3 | | |
| 4 | | |
| Total | | |

# Subtraction Bingo Activities

# Directions for Subtraction Bingo Activities

- Practice computing the differences of number combinations 1–18.
- Practice computing the difference between 65 and a number ending in 0 or 5.
- Reinforce the directionality concepts of diagonal, horizontal, and vertical.
- Develop cooperative skills by taking turns being the Bingo caller.

*Subtraction Bingo is a cooperative way to familiarize students with subtraction concepts. The simplicity of the activity makes it a tool for diversifying learning. Some students may find it beneficial to stay with this activity, switching cards after each round, to develop recognition and fluency.*

**Subtraction Bingo** may be played with 2–5 teams or players. Two teams with 2 students on a team are suggested. Playing on teams gives students an opportunity to discuss moves and strategies and provides a check on correct computation.

## Materials

- Dice
- Bingo cards (set of 5)
- Tokens (tiles, cubes, chips)

## How to Play

- Each team receives a Bingo card.
- Each team tosses a die. The team with the highest number designates a Bingo caller on that team. Players on the team take turns being the Bingo caller.
- The caller tosses a die or dice and calls out the number. All players agree on the solution to the subtraction problem.
- Teams place a token on one of the solutions on their card. If no play is possible, the team loses a turn.
- The first team to get Bingo (5 tokens in a row horizontally, vertically, or diagonally) is the winner.

## Suggestions

- Encourage students to think their way through subtraction as a mental activity. If they are subtracting 18 − 12, for example, have them first consider 18 − 10, which is an easier equation to solve. Explore what they would have to do to use the answer from 18 − 10 to solve 18 − 12.
- If students are struggling with subtraction facts, suggest that they use the Hundred Chart (page vi) to help them with their computation.

## Variations

- Teams place a token on all boxes containing the solution.
- The winning card must have Bingo diagonally and horizontally.
- The winning card must have Bingo diagonally and vertically.
- The winning card must have Bingo horizontally and vertically.

## Discussion

- Is this a game of luck or skill?
- How does playing Bingo help you learn subtraction facts?

- Each team tosses a die.
- Team with the highest number designates a Bingo caller on that team.
- Players on that team take turns as the Bingo caller.

**How to Play**

- Caller tosses a die and calls out the number.
- All players agree on 10 minus the value of the die. Teams look for this number on their Bingo card and place a token on it.
- If no play is possible, lose a turn.
- First team to get Bingo (5 in a row horizontally, vertically, or diagonally) is the winner.

**Card A**

# SUBTRACTION BINGO

| 9 | 5 | 7 | 6 | 8 |
|---|---|---|---|---|
| 6 | 4 | 8 | 4 | 7 |
| 5 | 9 | Free | 4 | 5 |
| 8 | 7 | 9 | 6 | 8 |
| 7 | 4 | 6 | 9 | 5 |

- Each team tosses a die.
- Team with the highest number designates a Bingo caller on that team.
- Players on that team take turns as the Bingo caller.

**How to Play**

- Caller tosses a die and calls out the number.
- All players agree on 10 minus the value of the die. Teams look for this number on their Bingo card and place a token on it.
- If no play is possible, lose a turn.
- First team to get Bingo (5 in a row horizontally, vertically, or diagonally) is the winner.

**Card B**

# SUBTRACTION BINGO

| 9 | 7 | 8 | 6 | 4 |
|---|---|---|---|---|
| 6 | 4 | 9 | 7 | 5 |
| 7 | 8 | Free | 5 | 4 |
| 9 | 5 | 6 | 4 | 8 |
| 8 | 6 | 7 | 9 | 5 |

- Each team tosses a die.
- Team with the highest number designates a Bingo caller on that team.
- Players on that team take turns as the Bingo caller.

**How to Play**

- Caller tosses a die and calls out the number.
- All players agree on 10 minus the value of the die. Teams look for this number on their Bingo card and place a token on it.
- If no play is possible, lose a turn.
- First team to get Bingo (5 in a row horizontally, vertically, or diagonally) is the winner.

**Card C**

# SUBTRACTION BINGO

| 9 | 4 | 7 | 5 | 8 |
|---|---|---|---|---|
| 9 | 5 | 8 | 6 | 5 |
| 7 | 4 | Free | 7 | 9 |
| 8 | 5 | 6 | 8 | 4 |
| 9 | 4 | 7 | 9 | 6 |

- *Each team tosses a die.*
- *Team with the highest number designates a Bingo caller on that team.*
- *Players on that team take turns as the Bingo caller.*

**How to Play**

- *Caller tosses a die and calls out the number.*
- *All players agree on 10 minus the value of the die. Teams look for this number on their Bingo card and place a token on it.*
- *If no play is possible, lose a turn.*
- *First team to get Bingo (5 in a row horizontally, vertically, or diagonally) is the winner.*

| Card D | SUBTRACTION BINGO | | | |
|:---:|:---:|:---:|:---:|:---:|
| 9 | 4 | 8 | 5 | 7 |
| 5 | 6 | 4 | 6 | 4 |
| 7 | 9 | Free | 7 | 4 |
| 8 | 5 | 6 | 8 | 9 |
| 7 | 9 | 8 | 5 | 6 |

- *Each team tosses a die.*
- *Team with the highest number designates a Bingo caller on that team.*
- *Players on that team take turns as the Bingo caller.*

- *Caller tosses a die and calls out the number.*
- *All players agree on 10 minus the value of the die. Teams look for this number on their Bingo card and place a token on it.*
- *If no play is possible, lose a turn.*
- *First team to get Bingo (5 in a row horizontally, vertically, or diagonally) is the winner.*

**Card E**

# SUBTRACTION BINGO

| 9 | 6 | 4 | 9 | 8 |
|---|---|---|---|---|
| 6 | 5 | 7 | 6 | 5 |
| 7 | 4 | Free | 7 | 8 |
| 5 | 8 | 4 | 5 | 9 |
| 8 | 4 | 7 | 9 | 6 |

- Each team tosses a die.
- Team with the highest number designates a Bingo caller on that team.
- Players on that team take turns as the Bingo caller.

**How to Play**

- Caller tosses two dice and calls out the sum of the dice.
- All players agree on 13 minus the sum of the dice. Teams look for this number on their Bingo card and place a token on it.
- If no play is possible, lose a turn.
- First team to get Bingo (5 in a row horizontally, vertically, or diagonally) is the winner.

**Card A**

# SUBTRACTION BINGO

| 12 | 3 | 7 | 4 | 5 |
|---|---|---|---|---|
| 6 | 1 | 4 | 8 | 4 |
| 2 | 5 | Free | 6 | 8 |
| 3 | 8 | 9 | 7 | 11 |
| 10 | 7 | 5 | 6 | 9 |

- Each team tosses a die.
- Team with the highest number designates a Bingo caller on that team.
- Players on that team take turns as the Bingo caller.

**How to Play**

- Caller tosses two dice and calls out the sum of the dice.
- All players agree on 13 minus the sum of the dice. Teams look for this number on their Bingo card and place a token on it.
- If no play is possible, lose a turn.
- First team to get Bingo (5 in a row horizontally, vertically, or diagonally) is the winner.

**Card B**

# SUBTRACTION BINGO

| 12 | 4 | 3 | 5 | 10 |
|----|----|------|----|----|
| 6 | 3 | 8 | 4 | 7 |
| 2 | 9 | Free | 1 | 5 |
| 8 | 7 | 11 | 6 | 8 |
| 7 | 4 | 6 | 9 | 5 |

- Each team tosses a die.
- Team with the highest number designates a Bingo caller on that team.
- Players on that team take turns as the Bingo caller.

**How to Play**

- Caller tosses two dice and calls out the sum of the dice.
- All players agree on 13 minus the sum of the dice. Teams look for this number on their Bingo card and place a token on it.
- If no play is possible, lose a turn.
- First team to get Bingo (5 in a row horizontally, vertically, or diagonally) is the winner.

**Card C**

# SUBTRACTION BINGO

| 12 | 4 | 6 | 8 | 3 |
|----|----|------|----|----|
| 7 | 9 | 3 | 11 | 5 |
| 5 | 4 | Free | 2 | 1 |
| 4 | 10 | 6 | 7 | 8 |
| 8 | 7 | 5 | 9 | 6 |

**How to Play**

- Each team tosses a die.
- Team with the highest number designates a Bingo caller on that team.
- Players on that team take turns as the Bingo caller.

- Caller tosses two dice and calls out the sum of the dice.
- All players agree on 13 minus the sum of the dice. Teams look for this number on their Bingo card and place a token on it.
- If no play is possible, lose a turn.
- First team to get Bingo (5 in a row horizontally, vertically, or diagonally) is the winner.

**Card D**

# SUBTRACTION BINGO

| 12 | 8 | 11 | 5 | 7 |
|----|----|------|----|----|
| 3 | 4 | 6 | 1 | 9 |
| 7 | 10 | Free | 6 | 8 |
| 5 | 6 | 8 | 7 | 4 |
| 9 | 2 | 5 | 4 | 3 |

- Each team tosses a die.
- Team with the highest number designates a Bingo caller on that team.
- Players on that team take turns as the Bingo caller.

**How to Play**

- Caller tosses two dice and calls out the sum of the dice.
- All players agree on 13 minus the sum of the dice. Teams look for this number on their Bingo card and place a token on it.
- If no play is possible, lose a turn.
- First team to get Bingo (5 in a row horizontally, vertically, or diagonally) is the winner.

| Card E | SUBTRACTION BINGO | | | |
|---|---|---|---|---|
| 12 | 3 | 9 | 6 | 11 |
| 8 | 5 | 4 | 2 | 7 |
| 6 | 8 | Free | 9 | 4 |
| 3 | 4 | 10 | 8 | 7 |
| 5 | 7 | 6 | 1 | 5 |

**How to Play**

- *Each team tosses a die.*
- *Team with the highest number designates a Bingo caller on that team.*
- *Players on that team take turns as the Bingo caller.*

- *Caller tosses two dice and calls out the sum of the dice.*
- *All players agree on 18 minus the sum of the dice. Teams look for this number on their Bingo card and place a token on it.*
- *If no play is possible, lose a turn.*
- *First team to get Bingo (5 in a row horizontally, vertically, or diagonally) is the winner.*

**Card A**

# SUBTRACTION BINGO

| 16 | 9 | 12 | 8 | 11 |
|----|----|------|----|----|
| 6 | 10 | 14 | 15 | 10 |
| 12 | 7 | Free | 13 | 8 |
| 15 | 11 | 9 | 7 | 11 |
| 10 | 13 | 16 | 6 | 14 |

**How to Play**

- Each team tosses a die.
- Team with the highest number designates a Bingo caller on that team.
- Players on that team take turns as the Bingo caller.

- Caller tosses two dice and calls out the sum of the dice.
- All players agree on 18 minus the sum of the dice. Teams look for this number on their Bingo card and place a token on it.
- If no play is possible, lose a turn.
- First team to get Bingo (5 in a row horizontally, vertically, or diagonally) is the winner.

**Card B**

# SUBTRACTION BINGO

| 16 | 8 | 11 | 12 | 15 |
|----|----|----|----|----|
| 6 | 13 | 7 | 9 | 14 |
| 15 | 8 | Free | 16 | 12 |
| 12 | 10 | 7 | 11 | 9 |
| 13 | 11 | 6 | 10 | 14 |

**How to Play**

- Each team tosses a die.
- Team with the highest number designates a Bingo caller on that team.
- Players on that team take turns as the Bingo caller.

- Caller tosses two dice and calls out the sum of the dice.
- All players agree on 18 minus the sum of the dice. Teams look for this number on their Bingo card and place a token on it.
- If no play is possible, lose a turn.
- First team to get Bingo (5 in a row horizontally, vertically, or diagonally) is the winner.

**Card C**

# SUBTRACTION BINGO

| 16 | 9 | 12 | 13 | 7 |
|----|----|------|----|----|
| 14 | 11 | 6 | 8 | 10 |
| 13 | 15 | Free | 9 | 12 |
| 8 | 11 | 7 | 10 | 6 |
| 10 | 16 | 12 | 15 | 14 |

**How to Play**

- Each team tosses a die.
- Team with the highest number designates a Bingo caller on that team.
- Players on that team take turns as the Bingo caller.

- Caller tosses two dice and calls out the sum of the dice.
- All players agree on 18 minus the sum of the dice. Teams look for this number on their Bingo card and place a token on it.
- If no play is possible, lose a turn.
- First team to get Bingo (5 in a row horizontally, vertically, or diagonally) is the winner.

**Card D**

# SUBTRACTION BINGO

| 16 | 8 | 14 | 10 | 6 |
|----|----|----|----|----|
| 13 | 12 | 15 | 9 | 11 |
| 15 | 10 | Free | 6 | 12 |
| 7 | 11 | 8 | 13 | 9 |
| 14 | 16 | 11 | 7 | 10 |

**How to Play**

- Each team tosses a die.
- Team with the highest number designates a Bingo caller on that team.
- Players on that team take turns as the Bingo caller.

- Caller tosses two dice and calls out the sum of the dice.
- All players agree on 18 minus the sum of the dice. Teams look for this number on their Bingo card and place a token on it.
- If no play is possible, lose a turn.
- First team to get Bingo (5 in a row horizontally, vertically, or diagonally) is the winner.

**Card E**

# SUBTRACTION BINGO

| 16 | 11 | 14 | 8 | 10 |
|----|----|----|----|----|
| 12 | 9 | 13 | 6 | 15 |
| 11 | 14 | Free | 7 | 12 |
| 10 | 6 | 8 | 16 | 9 |
| 15 | 12 | 13 | 11 | 7 |

## Subtraction Bingo

**How to Play**

- Each team tosses a die.
- Team with the highest number designates a Bingo caller on that team.
- Players on that team take turns as the Bingo caller.

- Each dot equals 5. The caller tosses a die, calls out the value of the die, and subtracts the value from **65**.
- All players agree on 65 minus the value of the die. Teams place a token on their Bingo card on one of the boxes that has the number.
- If no play is possible, lose a turn. First team to get Bingo (5 in a row horizontally, vertically, or diagonally) is the winner.

**Card A**

# SUBTRACTION BINGO

| 35 | 55 | 45 | 50 | 40 |
|----|----|----|----|----|
| 50 | 60 | 40 | 60 | 45 |
| 55 | 35 | Free | 60 | 55 |
| 40 | 45 | 35 | 50 | 40 |
| 45 | 55 | 50 | 35 | 60 |

- *Each team tosses a die.*
- *Team with the highest number designates a Bingo caller on that team.*
- *Players on that team take turns as the Bingo caller.*

- *Each dot equals 5. The caller tosses a die, calls out the value of the die, and subtracts the value from **65.***
- *All players agree on 65 minus the value of the die. Teams place a token on their Bingo card on one of the boxes that has the number.*
- *If no play is possible, lose a turn. First team to get Bingo (5 in a row horizontally, vertically, or diagonally) is the winner.*

**Card B**

# SUBTRACTION BINGO

| 35 | 45 | 40 | 50 | 55 |
|----|----|----|----|----|
| 60 | 55 | 35 | 45 | 60 |
| 45 | 40 | Free | 55 | 55 |
| 35 | 60 | 50 | 55 | 40 |
| 40 | 50 | 45 | 35 | 60 |

- Each team tosses a die.
- Team with the highest number designates a Bingo caller on that team.
- Players on that team take turns as the Bingo caller.

**How to Play**

- Each dot equals 5. The caller tosses a die, calls out the value of the die, and subtracts the value from **65**.
- All players agree on 65 minus the value of the die. Teams place a token on their Bingo card on one of the boxes that has the number.
- If no play is possible, lose a turn. First team to get Bingo (5 in a row horizontally, vertically, or diagonally) is the winner.

**Card C**

# SUBTRACTION BINGO

| 35 | 60 | 45 | 55 | 40 |
|----|----|----|----|----|
| 50 | 55 | 40 | 50 | 55 |
| 45 | 60 | Free | 45 | 35 |
| 40 | 55 | 50 | 40 | 60 |
| 35 | 60 | 45 | 35 | 50 |

## Subtraction Bingo

- Each team tosses a die.
- Team with the highest number designates a Bingo caller on that team.
- Players on that team take turns as the Bingo caller.

**How to Play**

- Each dot equals 5. The caller tosses a die, calls out the value of the die, and subtracts the value from **65.**
- All players agree on 65 minus the value of the die. Teams place a token on their Bingo card on one of the boxes that has the number.
- If no play is possible, lose a turn. First team to get Bingo (5 in a row horizontally, vertically, or diagonally) is the winner.

**Card D**

# SUBTRACTION BINGO

| 35 | 60 | 40 | 55 | 45 |
|----|----|----|----|----|
| 55 | 50 | 60 | 50 | 60 |
| 45 | 35 | Free | 45 | 60 |
| 40 | 55 | 50 | 40 | 35 |
| 45 | 35 | 40 | 55 | 50 |

- Each team tosses a die.
- Team with the highest number designates a Bingo caller on that team.
- Players on that team take turns as the Bingo caller.

- Each dot equals 5. The caller tosses a die, calls out the value of the die, and subtracts the value from **65**.
- All players agree on 65 minus the value of the die. Teams place a token on their Bingo card on one of the boxes that has the number.
- If no play is possible, lose a turn. First team to get Bingo (5 in a row horizontally, vertically, or diagonally) is the winner.

**Card E**

# SUBTRACTION BINGO

| 35 | 50 | 60 | 35 | 40 |
|----|----|----|----|----|
| 50 | 55 | 45 | 50 | 55 |
| 45 | 60 | Free | 45 | 40 |
| 55 | 40 | 60 | 55 | 35 |
| 40 | 60 | 45 | 35 | 50 |

| SUBTRACTION BINGO | | | | |
|---|---|---|---|---|
|  |  |  |  |  |
|  |  |  |  |  |
|  |  | Free |  |  |
|  |  |  |  |  |
|  |  |  |  |  |

# Hidden Number Activities

# Directions for Hidden Number Activities

## Objectives

- Develop short-term memory and visual discrimination.
- Develop a sense of number and number patterns when subtracting numbers 1 through 20.
- Recognize number patterns when subtracting from a two-digit number ending in 0.
- Recognize number patterns when subtracting 10 from a two-digit number ending in 0 or 5.
- Encourage students to trust their memory as a strategy.

Introduce **Hidden Number** activities by demonstrating on an overhead or gathering the students together on a rug and playing against the class.

Two teams with two students on a team are suggested. Playing as teams gives students an opportunity to discuss moves and strategies and provides a check on correct computation.

## Materials

- Dice
- Hidden number chart
- Tiles, chips, or Unifix cubes (big enough to completely cover the numerals on the chart)

## How to Play

- Cover each number on the chart with a tile.
- Each team tosses a die. The higher number goes first.
- On each turn, one team tosses a die or two dice and performs the required computation.

### 3 × 4 Charts Using a Die or Two Dice
### 5 × 5 Charts Using a Die

- The team removes a tile to see if the number on the chart is the same as the solution. If there is a match, the team removes the tile and tosses again. If the number is not a match, the team replaces the tile and the turn ends.
- When all tiles have been removed from the chart, the team with the most tiles wins.

## 5 × 5 Charts Using Two Dice

- *In this version, the teams remove two tiles with each toss.* If the first number uncovered is a match, the team removes the tile and takes another turn.
- If the first number uncovered is not a match, the team replaces the tile and removes another.
- If the second number uncovered is a match, the team takes another turn.
- If second number is not a match, the team replaces the tile and the turn ends.
- When all tiles have been removed from the chart, the team with the most tiles wins.

## Variations

- If the game is not progressing, suggest that teams each make 5 more tosses. If after 5 tosses, tiles still remain on the chart, end the game. The team with the most tiles wins.

## Discussion

- What techniques do you use to help you remember the hidden numbers?

# 10 Minus a Die
## Hidden Number

**How to Play**

- Teacher covers the numbers on the Hidden Number Chart with color tiles, chips, or Unifix Cubes.
- Each team tosses a die. Higher number goes first.

- Toss a die and subtract the number from **10.**
- Remove a tile to see if the number on the chart matches the solution. If it matches, play again.
- If the number you uncovered does not match, replace the tile and your team's turn ends.
- Teams take turns until all tiles are removed. Team with the most tiles wins.

| | | |
|---|---|---|
| 6 | 8 | 7 |
| 9 | 4 | 6 |
| 5 | 7 | 5 |
| 8 | 4 | 9 |

**How to Play**

- Teacher covers the numbers on the Hidden Number Chart with color tiles, chips, or Unifix Cubes.
- Each team tosses a die. Higher number goes first.

- Toss a die and subtract the number from **10.**
- Remove a tile to see if the number on the chart matches the solution. If it matches, play again.
- If the number you uncovered does not match, replace the tile and your team's turn ends.
- Teams take turns until all tiles are removed. The team with the most tiles wins.

| 4 | 6 | 5 | 9 | 8 |
|---|---|---|---|---|
| 5 | 7 | 6 | 4 | 9 |
| 7 | 8 | 9 | 5 | 7 |
| 8 | 9 | 4 | 7 | 6 |
| 6 | 5 | 7 | 8 | 4 |

**How to Play**

- Teacher covers the numbers on the Hidden Number Chart with color tiles, chips, or Unifix Cubes.

- Each team tosses a die. Higher number goes first.

- Toss 2 dice and find the sum. Subtract the sum from **15**.

- Remove one tile to see if the number on the chart matches the solution. If it matches, play again. If the number you uncovered does not match, replace the tile and your team's turn ends.

- Teams take turns until all tiles are removed. Team with the most tiles wins.

| | | |
|:---:|:---:|:---:|
| **6** | **8** | **11** |
| **9** | **13** | **8** |
| **3** | **7** | **5** |
| **10** | **4** | **12** |

# 15 Minus Two-Dice-Sum Hidden Number

**How to Play**

- Teacher covers the numbers on the Hidden Number Chart with color tiles, chips, or Unifix Cubes.
- Each team tosses a die. Higher number goes first.

- Toss 2 dice and find the sum. Subtract the sum from **15.**
- Remove one tile to see if the number on the chart matches the solution. If it matches, play again.
- If the number you uncovered does not match, replace the tile and remove another tile.
- If the second number matches, play again. If it doesn't match, replace that tile and your team's turn ends.
- Teams take turns until all tiles are removed. Team with the most tiles wins.

| | | | | |
|---|---|---|---|---|
| **9** | **5** | **4** | **6** | **8** |
| **10** | **7** | **11** | **9** | **12** |
| **8** | **12** | **7** | **6** | **10** |
| **7** | **3** | **8** | **13** | **5** |
| **11** | **9** | **6** | **10** | **4** |

**How to Play**

- Teacher covers the numbers on the Hidden Number Chart with color tiles, chips, or Unifix Cubes.
- Each team tosses a die. Higher number goes first.

- Toss 2 dice and find the sum. Subtract the sum from **20.**
- Remove one tile to see if the number on the chart matches the solution. If it matches, play again. If the number you uncovered does not match, replace the tile and your team's turn ends.
- Teams take turns until all tiles are removed. Team with the most tiles wins.

| | | |
|---|---|---|
| **11** | **13** | **16** |
| **14** | **18** | **8** |
| **13** | **12** | **10** |
| **15** | **9** | **17** |

# 20 Minus Two-Dice-Sum Hidden Number

**How to Play**

- Teacher covers the numbers on the Hidden Number Chart with color tiles, chips, or Unifix Cubes.
- Each team tosses a die. Higher number goes first.

- Toss 2 dice and find the sum. Subtract the sum from **20.**
- Remove one tile to see if the number on the chart matches the solution. If it matches, play again.
- If the number you uncovered does not match, replace the tile and remove another tile.
- If the second number matches, play again. If it doesn't match, replace that tile and your team's turn ends.
- Teams take turns until all tiles are removed. Team with the most tiles wins.

| | | | | |
|---|---|---|---|---|
| **9** | **18** | **15** | **17** | **8** |
| **18** | **16** | **11** | **14** | **13** |
| **14** | **12** | **17** | **12** | **10** |
| **11** | **16** | **8** | **13** | **14** |
| **13** | **9** | **12** | **10** | **15** |

# 100 Minus a Tens Die Hidden Number

| 60 | 80 | 70 |
|----|----|----|
| 90 | 40 | 60 |
| 50 | 70 | 50 |
| 80 | 40 | 90 |

# 100 Minus a Tens Die Hidden Number

**How to Play**

- Teacher covers the numbers on the Hidden Number Chart with color tiles, chips, or Unifix Cubes.
- Each team tosses a die. Higher number goes first.

- Toss a die. Each dot on the die equals 10. Count by tens to find the value of the die. Subtract the value from **100.**
- Remove one tile to see if the number on the chart matches the solution. If it matches, play again.
- If the number you uncovered does not match, replace the tile and remove another tile.
- If the second number matches, play again. If it doesn't match, replace that tile and your team's turn ends.
- Teams take turns until all tiles are removed. Team with the most tiles wins.

| 40 | 60 | 50 | 90 | 80 |
|----|----|----|----|----|
| 50 | 70 | 60 | 40 | 90 |
| 70 | 80 | 90 | 50 | 70 |
| 80 | 90 | 40 | 70 | 60 |
| 60 | 50 | 70 | 80 | 40 |

**How to Play**

- Teacher covers the numbers on the Hidden Number Chart with color tiles, chips, or Unifix Cubes.

- Each team tosses a die. Higher number goes first.

- Toss a die. Each dot on the die equals 10. Count by tens to find the value of the die. Subtract the value from **65**.

- Remove a tile to see if the number on the chart matches the solution. If it matches, play again.

- If the number you uncovered does not match, replace the tile and your team's turn ends.

- Teams take turns until all tiles are removed. Team with the most tiles wins.

| | | |
|:---:|:---:|:---:|
| **25** | **45** | **35** |
| **55** | **5** | **25** |
| **15** | **35** | **15** |
| **45** | **5** | **55** |

# 65 Minus a Tens Die Hidden Number

| 5 | 25 | 15 | 55 | 45 |
|---|----|----|----|----|
| 15 | 35 | 25 | 5 | 55 |
| 35 | 45 | 55 | 15 | 35 |
| 45 | 55 | 5 | 35 | 25 |
| 25 | 15 | 35 | 45 | 5 |

|  |  |  |
|---|---|---|
|  |  |  |
|  |  |  |
|  |  |  |
|  |  |  |

|  |  |  |  |  |
|--|--|--|--|--|
|  |  |  |  |  |
|  |  |  |  |  |
|  |  |  |  |  |
|  |  |  |  |  |
|  |  |  |  |  |

# Tic-Tac-Toe / Four-Grid Tic-Tac-Toe Activities

# Directions for Tic-Tac-Toe/ Four-Grid Tic-Tac-Toe Activities

- Practice computing the difference between number combinations 1–25.
- Recognize patterns when subtracting a multiple of 5 (5 to 30) from two-digit numbers ending in 0.
- Develop communication and cooperation skills by working in teams of two students.
- Recognize the advantage of employing a defense strategy.

*Tic-Tac-Toe* is a familiar game form. These Tic-Tac-Toe activities provide a challenging and playful variation to use in practicing subtraction facts.

Each *Tic-Tac-Toe* activity is paired with a *Four-Grid Tic-Tac-Toe* activity, providing a way to diversify while reinforcing specific mathematical concepts. This format presents opportunities for students to practice each of the mathematical concepts playing *Tic-Tac-Toe* before moving on to the more complicated *Four-Grid Tic-Tac-Toe*.

Two teams with two students on a team are suggested. Playing as teams gives students an opportunity to discuss moves and strategies and provides a check on correct computation.

## Materials

- Chart
- Dice
- Tokens (tiles, chips, cubes)

## Warm-Up Activity: *Tic-Tac-Toe*

- Introduce the *Tic-Tac-Toe* activities by demonstrating a standard game of Tic-Tac-Toe, using Xs and Os and playing against the class.

## Discussion

- Does the side that goes first have an advantage?
- Is this a game of luck or skill?
- Is it a fair game?

## How to Play: *Tic-Tac-Toe*

- Each team chooses a token and tosses a die. The higher number goes first.
- Taking turns, teams toss a die or dice, depending on the activity, and perform the required subtraction.
- With each toss of the die or dice, teams attempt to place their tokens in continuous alignment, vertically, horizontally, or diagonally, to win the game.
- If the solution is not shown on the grid or the number already has a token on it, the team loses a turn.
- The first team to form a Tic-Tac-Toe wins the game.
- The team winning 2 out of 3 games is the winner.

## Suggestions

- Encourage students to think their way through subtraction as a mental activity. If they are subtracting 25 – 8, for example, have them first consider 25 – 10, which is an easier equation to solve. Explore what they would have to do to use the answer from 25 – 10 to solve 25 – 8.
- If students are struggling with subtraction facts, suggest that they use the Hundred Chart (page vi) to help them with their calculations.

## Variations

- Teams place a token on every box in which the solution appears.
- Teams replace the opponent's token with their own token on their turn.

## Discussion

- Does the dice toss influence your strategy?
- Does the dice toss influence the outcome of the game?
- Is there a fair chance of each solution being tossed?
- Is this a fair game?

## How to Play:
### Four-Grid Tic-Tac-Toe

Introduce the **Four-Grid Tic-Tac-Toe** activity by demonstrating it on an overhead and playing against the class.

- Each team chooses a token and tosses a die. The higher number goes first.
- Taking turns, teams toss the die or dice, depending on the activity, and perform the required computation.
- Teams locate the solution on any of the Tic-Tac-Toe grids and place a token on only one of the solutions.

- With each toss of the die or dice, teams attempt to place their tokens in a continuous alignment, vertically, horizontally, or diagonally, forming as many Tic-Tac-Toe wins as possible.
- If the solution is not shown on the grid or the solution already has a token on it, the team loses a turn.
- When no more plays are possible, both teams count their Tic-Tac-Toe wins. The team with the most Tic-Tac-Toes wins the game.

## Variations

- Team places a token on every box in which the solution appears on all four Tic-Tac-Toe grids.
- The teams agree to both use the same strategy to see what happens.
- The teams agree to each use a different strategy to see what happens.

## Discussion

- What was your strategy in trying to win? Were you playing offensively or defensively? Did you play on one grid at a time, or did you play on all four grids simultaneously?
- Which strategy works best: trying to get the most three tokens in a row or trying to block your opponent?
- Discuss what might happen if both teams agreed to use the same strategy.
- Discuss what might happen if the two teams agreed to each use a different strategy and let the opposing team know what their strategy would be (playing offensively or defensively).

# 10 Minus a Die Tic-Tac-Toe

- *Each team tosses a die. Higher number goes first.*
- *Each team chooses a color token.*

**How to Play**

- *Toss a die. Subtract the number from **10**.*
- *Place a token on the difference.*
- *If the number already has a token on it, lose a turn.*
- *First team to get three tokens in a row wins.*
- *Play 3 games. Team winning 2 out of 3 games wins.*

| | | |
|:---:|:---:|:---:|
| **7** | **8** | **5** |
| **5** | **6** | **7** |
| **8** | **9** | **4** |

- Each team tosses a die. Higher number goes first.
- Each team chooses a color token.

**How to Play**

- Toss a die. Subtract the number from **10.**
- Find the difference on any of the Tic-Tac-Toe grids and place a token on it.
- If the number is not available on any grid, lose a turn.
- Team with the most "three tokens in a row" wins.

| | | | | | | |
|---|---|---|---|---|---|---|
| 6 | 7 | 4 | | 7 | 5 | 9 |
| 4 | 8 | 9 | | 8 | 6 | 4 |
| 5 | 7 | 5 | | 9 | 5 | 7 |
| | | | | | | |
| 9 | 4 | 8 | | 4 | 6 | 8 |
| 7 | 5 | 9 | | 9 | 7 | 6 |
| 6 | 8 | 6 | | 5 | 4 | 8 |

- Each team tosses a die. Higher number goes first.
- Each team chooses a color token.

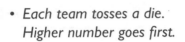

**How to Play**

- Toss 2 dice. Find the sum. Subtract the sum from **13.**
- Find the difference on the grid and place a token on it.
- If the number is not available, lose a turn.
- First team to get three tokens in a row wins.
- Play 3 games. Team winning 2 out of 3 games wins.

| | | |
|---|---|---|
| 7 | 8 | 2 |
| 5 | 6 | 10 |
| 3 | 9 | 4 |

- Each team tosses a die. Higher number goes first.
- Each team chooses a color token.

**How to Play**

- Toss 2 dice. Find the sum. Subtract the sum from **13.**
- Place a token on the difference on any of the Tic-Tac-Toe grids.
- If the number is not available on any grid, lose a turn.
- Team with the most "three tokens in a row" wins.

| | | | | | | |
|---|---|---|---|---|---|---|
| 6 | 7 | 4 | | 3 | 5 | 2 |
| 3 | 8 | 9 | | 8 | 6 | 4 |
| 5 | 7 | 10 | | 9 | 5 | 7 |
| | | | | | | |
| 9 | 4 | 10 | | 2 | 6 | 8 |
| 7 | 5 | 1 | | 3 | 7 | 6 |
| 6 | 8 | 6 | | 5 | 4 | 11 |

- *Each team tosses a die. Higher number goes first.*
- *Each team chooses a color token.*

**How to Play**

- *Toss 2 dice. Find the sum. Subtract the sum from **25**.*
- *Find the difference on the grid and place a token on it.*
- *If the number already has a token on it, lose a turn.*
- *First team to get three tokens in a row wins.*
- *Play 3 games. Team winning 2 out of 3 games wins.*

| | | |
|:---:|:---:|:---:|
| **19** | **20** | **14** |
| **17** | **18** | **22** |
| **15** | **21** | **16** |

- *Each team tosses a die. Higher number goes first.*
- *Each team chooses a color token.*

**How to Play**

- *Toss 2 dice. Find the sum. Subtract the sum from **25**.*
- *Place a token on the difference on any of the Tic-Tac-Toe grids.*
- *If the number is not available on any grid, lose a turn.*
- *Team with the most "three tokens in a row" wins.*

| | | | | | | |
|---|---|---|---|---|---|---|
| **18** | **19** | **17** | | **15** | **17** | **14** |
| **15** | **20** | **21** | | **20** | **18** | **16** |
| **16** | **19** | **22** | | **21** | **17** | **19** |
| | | | | | | |
| **21** | **16** | **22** | | **14** | **18** | **20** |
| **19** | **17** | **13** | | **15** | **19** | **18** |
| **18** | **20** | **18** | | **17** | **16** | **23** |

# 30 Minus a Fives Die Tic-Tac-Toe

**How to Play**

- Each team tosses a die. Higher number goes first.
- Each team chooses a color token.

- Toss a die. Each dot equals 5. Count by fives to find the value of the die.
- Subtract the die value from **30**.
- Find the difference on the grid and place a token on it.
- If the number already has a token on it, lose a turn.
- First team to get three tokens in a row wins.
- Play 3 games. Team winning 2 out of 3 games wins.

| | | |
|:---:|:---:|:---:|
| **15** | **25** | **10** |
| **0** | **5** | **20** |
| **15** | **10** | **25** |

- Each team tosses a die. Higher number goes first.
- Each team chooses a color token.

**How to Play**

- Toss a die. Each dot equals 5. Count by fives to find the value of the die.
- Subtract the die value from **30**.
- Find the difference on any of the Tic-Tac-Toe grids and place a token on it.
- If the number is not available on any grid, lose a turn.
- Team with the most "three tokens in a row" wins.

| 15 | 25 | 0 | | 20 | 5 | 10 |
|----|----|----|----|----|----|----|
| 25 | 5 | 20 | | 10 | 15 | 0 |
| 10 | 0 | 15 | | 20 | 0 | 25 |
| | | | | | | |
| 10 | 20 | 5 | | 10 | 25 | 5 |
| 5 | 25 | 15 | | 15 | 20 | 0 |
| 20 | 0 | 10 | | 25 | 5 | 15 |

# 100 Minus a Fives Die Tic-Tac-Toe

**How to Play**

- Each team tosses a die. Higher number goes first.
- Each team chooses a color token.

- Toss a die. Each dot equals 5. Count by fives to find the value of the die.
- Subtract the die value from **100.**
- Find the difference on the grid and place a token on it.
- If the number already has a token on it, lose a turn.
- First team to get three tokens in a row wins.
- Play 3 games. Team winning 2 out of 3 games wins.

| | | |
|---|---|---|
| **70** | **75** | **90** |
| **90** | **85** | **70** |
| **75** | **80** | **95** |